GROUP
→ *Video Experience* ←

TONY EVANS
KINGDOM
STEWARDSHIP

MANAGING ALL OF LIFE
UNDER GOD'S RULE

TYNDALE HOUSE PUBLISHERS
CAROL STREAM, ILLINOIS

FOCUS ON THE FAMILY®

Kingdom Stewardship Group Video Experience Participant's Guide

Copyright © 2020 Focus on the Family. All rights reserved.

Based on the book *Kingdom Stewardship* by Dr. Tony Evans, © 2020 Tony Evans. Published by Tyndale House Publishers and Focus on the Family.

A Focus on the Family book published by Tyndale House Publishers, Carol Stream, Illinois 60188

Focus on the Family and the accompanying logo and design are federally registered trademarks of Focus on the Family, 8605 Explorer Drive, Colorado Springs, CO 80920.

TYNDALE and Tyndale's quill logo are registered trademarks of Tyndale House Publishers.

Portions of this book are adapted from *Living in Financial Victory* by Tony Evans (Chicago: Moody Publishers, 2013). Used by permission.

All Scriptures quotations, unless otherwise marked, are taken from the *New American Standard Bible*®. Copyright © 1960, 1962, 1963, 1968, 1971, 1972, 1973, 1975, 1977, 1995 by The Lockman Foundation. Used by permission. (www.Lockman.org).

Scripture quotations marked (ESV) are taken from *The Holy Bible, English Standard Version*. Copyright © 2001 by CrosswayBibles, a publishing ministry of Good News Publishers. Used by permission. All rights reserved.

Cover design by Sally Dunn

Cover image copyright © iStockphoto//PeopleImages. All rights reserved.

For information about special discounts for bulk purchases, please contact Tyndale House Publishers at csresponse@tyndale.com, or call 1-800-323-9400.

Library of Congress Control Number: 2019949732

ISBN 978-1-58997-831-7

Printed in the United States of America

26	25	24	23	22	21	20
7	6	5	4	3	2	

CONTENTS

Welcome, Kingdom Stewards!

At the core of this unique look at stewardship is this truth: You are the executive manager over all God has given to you!

Kingdom stewardship is the divinely authorized responsibility for believers to faithfully oversee the protection and expansion of the assets (time, talents, and treasures) God has entrusted to them to manage on His behalf.

Kingdom stewards are believers who faithfully oversee the protection and expansion of the assets God has entrusted to them to manage on His behalf.

This participant's guide will help you explore in rich, biblical detail how to manage all of life under the rule and authority of God. You'll discover the abundance and satisfaction of a life lived for God.

At the core of each session is a video presentation featuring Dr. Tony Evans, author of *Kingdom Stewardship*. Dr. Evans' inspired teaching will give every participant new insights into biblical principles as well as assurances that God has established a pathway to greater blessing and reward through the right management (stewardship) of all He has given to you.

To make these truths come alive, you'll find these sections in each session:

The Gathering

Read the key Scripture verse, the Main Point, and a brief excerpt from the book *Kingdom Stewardship*. Answer the questions that follow the excerpt. If you run out of time, finish the section at home.

Show Time!

Use this section as you view and think about the DVD presentation; it includes thought-provoking questions and biblical input.

Transformation Moments

This wrap-up, which focuses on applicable Scripture passages, will help you find encouragement and ideas for applying the teaching to your own life.

Note: The DVD presentations and this guide are intended as general advice only, and are not meant to replace clinical counseling, medical treatment, legal counsel, or pastoral guidance.

Focus on the Family maintains a referral network of Christian counselors. For information, call 1-855-771-HELP (4357) or contact FocusOnTheFamily.com/Counseling.

1

THE RESPONSIBILITY

His master said to him, "Well done, good and faithful servant. You have been faithful over a little; I will set you over much. Enter into the joy of your master."

MATTHEW 25:23, ESV

The Main Point

The responsibility of kingdom stewards is to manage well what God has given them.

The Gathering

Begin your time together with prayer and praise. Seek to create a community of connection within your group by sharing prayer requests and experiences that provide members with an opportunity to engage with one another.

To find out more about the kingdom steward's management role, read the following excerpt from *Kingdom Stewardship*. Then discuss the question that appears at the end of the excerpt.

THIS IS GOD'S HOUSE

In football, you will often read or hear the phrase "This is our house" or "Defend the house!" What this means is that when a visiting team comes to play, the home team makes it known that the visitors have entered into their domain. The home team makes it clear that they plan to protect, defend, and rule their house. The goal is to send the visiting team back to their own house with a defeat.

While sayings like that in sports can often be chalked up to mere hype (after all, many home teams lose games in "their house"), when God makes a similar claim to His own creation—He speaks seriously. Psalm 24:1 states it clearly, "The earth is the LORD's, and all it contains, the world, and those who dwell in it." God claims comprehensive kingdom ownership over all creation. This is His house. This is His kingdom. We live in His domain.

Psalm 89:11 puts it this way, "The heavens are Yours, the earth also is Yours; the world and all it contains, You have founded them."

Revelation 4:11 states, "Worthy are You, our Lord and our God, to receive glory and honor and power; for You created all things, and because of Your will they existed, and were created."

God owns it all. And since God owns it all, neither you nor I have any right to claim ownership of something that is not ours. Even if we did make that claim, it wouldn't make any real difference just as it wouldn't make any real difference if I claimed that any of the houses we watched during seminary were mine. When the true owners returned, I'd be kicked to the curb and undoubtedly I wouldn't even receive the payment that was due me for house-sitting. No owner is going to stand by while someone else seeks to take what is theirs.

Neither will God stand by as His creatures seek to usurp His sovereignty and role as the rightful owner of all of creation.

There is no shared ownership in God's kingdom.

There are no partnerships or additional signatories on any deeds or titles.

God owns it all.

Once you clearly understand and apply that spiritual truth to your life, you have set yourself on a journey of understanding as well as a pathway of unleashing your fullest potential.[1]

Reflection and Discussion

How does knowing that God owns it all affect your understanding of your role in this world?

Show Time!

In session 1 of the *Kingdom Stewardship Group Video Experience*, Dr. Tony Evans explains what it means for people to be stewards of God's assets.

After viewing Tony Evans' presentation "The Responsibility," use the following questions to help you think through what you saw and heard.

1. In the business world, what are the concerns and responsibilities of a business owner?

   What are the concerns and responsibilities of a business manager?

2. If God is the owner of all things, what do you think are the concerns and responsibilities of God?

If we are the managers of what God owns, what should our concerns and responsibilities be?

3. Dr. Evans said that we are to act on God's behalf, protecting and expanding God's assets. What does it mean to act on God's behalf?

4. Dr. Evans says that conflict happens when managers start acting like owners. In what ways do people act more like owners than managers of God's assets?

What problems does that cause?

5. Dr. Evans teaches that God entrusts us with time, talents, and treasures. In what ways does a responsible kingdom steward manage the time God has given?

In what ways does a responsible kingdom steward manage the talents God has given?

In what ways does a responsible kingdom steward manage the treasures God has given?

6. Read Matthew 25:14-30. God expects us not just to protect the assets He's entrusted to us, but to grow those assets. What can you do this week to be a better steward?

For what purpose are we to grow what God has given to us?

7. How does God respond when we act as responsible kingdom stewards?

How have you experienced this in your life?

8. Dr. Evans stated that life changes when we realize that everything we have is given by God and that we are to manage it for His purposes. He says when we act as responsible kingdom stewards, we will be working in cooperation with God rather than in conflict with Him. What do you think would happen in your life if you were working in cooperation with God in this way?

Transformation Moments

Read the following passages. Answer the questions that follow. If you run out of time, finish this section at home.

> The earth is the LORD's, and all it contains, the world, and those who dwell in it.
>
> PSALM 24:1

Is there an area of your life where you need to apply God's overarching rule as His steward?

> God blessed them; and God said to them, "Be fruitful and multiply, and fill the earth, and subdue it; and rule over the fish of the sea and over the birds of the sky and over every living thing that moves on the earth."
>
> GENESIS 1:28

In what way can you demonstrate more personal responsibility in your sphere of influence to bring God glory?

Therefore be careful how you walk, not as unwise men but as wise, making the most of your time, because the days are evil.

EPHESIANS 5:15-16

Spend a moment conducting a personal time assessment. Is there something you could cut back on or remove altogether that would free up time to be spent more wisely for God's kingdom purposes?

Final Challenge

When you act as a responsible kingdom steward, you will experience the blessing of working in cooperation with God rather than in conflict with Him. In prayer this week, ask God to help you be fruitful and multiply the time, talents, and treasures He has given to you.

2

✿

THE COVENANT

But you shall remember the LORD your God, for it is He who is giving
you power to make wealth, that He may confirm His covenant which
He swore to your fathers, as it is this day.

DEUTERONOMY 8:18

The Main Point

God calls us to live as kingdom stewards in order to confirm His
covenant with us.

The Gathering

Begin your time together with prayer and praise. Seek to create a
community of connection within your group by sharing prayer
requests and experiences that provide members with an opportunity to engage with one another.

To find out more about the covenant between God and His
people, read the following excerpt from *Kingdom Stewardship*.
Then discuss the questions that appear at the end of the excerpt.

COVENANT LIVING

God's covenant is a love thing. He loves you. It's His love that initiated His creation and redemption of mankind. When you lose sight of the driving motivation behind His covenant with you, you limit the movement of the King in your circumstances. You will see His commands as rules to be kept rather than wisdom to protect you. As Scripture states, "For this is the love of God, that we keep His commandments; and His commandments are not burdensome" (1 John 5:3).

Far too many Christians are living lives of defeat because they don't realize God's commandments come from a heart of love. As a result, they operate outside of the covenant. Any time you are functioning apart from complete obedience to God's commands, you are out of alignment. In other words, if what you are doing, saying, or thinking is not what God wants, you are out of alignment with the covenant. It doesn't matter how you choose to justify your actions or words, or even if they make perfect logical sense to you. If what you do and what God says disagree, you're out of alignment with the covenant and, therefore, you're experiencing a diminished relationship with the living God.

Alignment in the structure of the covenant is critical to God confirming and validating His work and kingdom purposes in your life. There exists a causal relationship in covenantal blessings.

Unless you comprehend, believe, and apply that foundational truth to your approach of kingdom stewardship, nothing else I have to say in this book will amount to much more than a hill of beans for you. In fact, if you choose not to believe that foundational truth, you might as well close the book and stick it back on the shelf. Living under the rule of God in His covenantal structure is the primary root of everything else that follows. You cannot operate outside of His commandments and simultaneously operate as a kingdom steward. The two are mutually exclusive.[1]

Reflection and Discussion

Why is it so important for the kingdom steward to live in alignment with God's commands? What happens when we disregard God's commands?

Show Time!

In session 2 of the *Kingdom Stewardship Group Video Experience*, Dr. Tony Evans explains how living under the rule of God in His covenantal structure provides the foundation for covenantal blessings.

After viewing Tony Evans' presentation "The Covenant," use the following questions to help you think through what you saw and heard.

1. A covenant is a divinely created bond between two people. In a covenant, there are expectations for both parties. Marriage is an example of a covenant. What are the expectations of both parties in marriage?

2. There is also a covenant between God and Christians. What are the expectations for both parties in this covenant?

3. Read 1 Corinthians 6:19-20. In what ways is stewardship of all of life part of the covenant between God and His people?

4. Dr. Evans states that the covenant is the administrative mechanism of the kingdom and that God does His kingdom work through His covenant. Explain how God accomplishes His work through the covenantal agreement He has with His people.

5. Tony Evans likens the covenant to an umbrella. The kingdom steward who lives by the covenant is covered by the umbrella. Explain what it means for the kingdom steward to live under the umbrella of the covenant.

What are the benefits of living under the covenant?

6. Some choose not to live by the covenant. These people are not covered by the umbrella. What does this mean? In what ways do people live outside of the covenant?

7. Dr. Evans uses several word pictures to illustrate the concept of not living under the covenant. Discuss each word picture and consider how it helps you understand the importance of living under the covenant.

- A rebellious child who doesn't live by the rules of the house

- A car with tires that are out of alignment

- Idolatry: living by a false covenant by making an agreement with a false god

8. Conflict occurs when the parties in a covenant do not keep their side of the agreement. God always keeps His side of the covenant. But people frequently do not. Describe what conflict may look like in this situation.

9. Consider how you live under the covenant and how you fail to live under the covenant. How can you better align yourself under the umbrella of God's covenant this week?

How do you think this will benefit you?

Transformation Moments

Read the following passages. Answer the questions that follow. If you run out of time, finish this section at home.

> Beware that you do not forget the LORD your God by not keeping His commandments and His ordinances and His statutes which I am commanding you today.
>
> DEUTERONOMY 8:11

What does it look like to forget God?

> But you shall remember the LORD your God, for it is He who is giving you power to make wealth, that He may confirm His covenant which He swore to your fathers, as it is this day.
>
> DEUTERONOMY 8:18

What does it mean to remember God?

> For this is the love of God, that we keep His commandments;
> and His commandments are not burdensome.
>
> I JOHN 5:3

Do you view God's commandments as burdensome? In what way
can you see God's love reflected through His commandments?

Final Challenge

Meditate on the Scriptures covered in this week's session. Ask
God to reveal to you how He wants you to align your thoughts,
words, and actions under His covenantal rule in greater obedience
to His commands.

3

🌿

THE SPHERES

*The LORD bless you from Zion, and may you see the prosperity of Jerusalem all the
days of your life. Indeed, may you see your children's children. Peace be upon Israel!*

PSALM 128:5-6

The Main Point

Kingdom stewards align themselves under God's rule in the four
spheres of life: individual, family, church, and community.

The Gathering

Begin your time together with prayer and praise. Seek to create a
community of connection within your group by sharing prayer
requests and experiences that provide members with an opportunity to engage with one another.

To find out more about aligning oneself under God's rule, read
the following excerpt from *Kingdom Stewardship*. Then discuss the
questions that appear at the end of the excerpt.

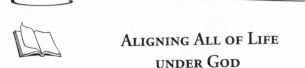

ALIGNING ALL OF LIFE
UNDER GOD

We live in a day when people are borrowing rules from society that do not agree with the rules of the owner. They are spending an inordinate amount of time gleaning rules from talk radio, reality shows, entertainment, and social media. This "babble-by-the-hour" has permeated the worldview of our society so much that it has become difficult to even recognize the presence of Christian values in our culture. Truth has been undermined. Everyone has their own version of truth. This used to be known as opinions, but somehow each person is now entitled to formulating their own set of truths by which to live. This has happened many times throughout history and it never ends up good (see Judges 21:25).

It's only when we abide by and operate under the structure of God's overarching rule that we will experience the benefits of His blessings and favor in our lives. Knowing and understanding His rules is the first step toward following them, so in this chapter I want to take a look at the four covenantal stewardship spheres within which God has organized the expression of His rule. Psalm 128 summarizes these four spheres of God's covenantal expression, breaking down His rule into its irreducible minimum. No area of your life sits outside these four realms. Remember that a covenant is a divinely created relational bond. It's an official agreement arranged and established by God through which His kingdom values are to be understood, yielded to, and followed. There's one more thing you must understand before we look at these four covenantal stewardship spheres. At some point there will be a big payday where you will receive a reward for how you managed life in these realms. We see the reference to the results of proper management pop up time and again in this passage of Psalm 128. It shows up as the word "blessed." We read:

How blessed is everyone who fears the LORD. (verse 1)
Behold, for thus shall the man be blessed. (verse 4)
The LORD bless you from Zion. (verse 5)

To speak of a blessing is to speak of divine favor. A blessing includes experiencing, enjoying, and extending the goodness of God in your life. The act of obtaining blessings in your life is directly tied to how well you manage or steward what God has entrusted you with.

Far too many people want God to bless them while they go about changing the rules in His house. They seek divine favor all the while piggybacking on the rules of the enemy. Praying for a blessing does not equate to receiving that blessing. Blessings are frequently tied to your alignment under God's rule. As a matter of fact, the word "bless" in Psalm 128 is directly tied to operating within your managerial responsibility according to God's will. When you truly grasp that truth, and apply it to how you think, decide, and react, you will begin to witness the favor of God showing up in four covenantal spheres of your life like you never even imagined He would.

The four spheres of stewardship mentioned in Psalm 128 are the individual, the family, the church, and the community, and each sphere has an economic benefit to it when it operates properly underneath God's kingdom rule.[1]

Reflection and Discussion

Dr. Evans teaches that blessings are tied to your alignment under God's rule. Explain what Dr. Evans means by blessings. How does this teaching affect your understanding of stewardship and its rewards?

Show Time!

In session 3 of the *Kingdom Stewardship Group Video Experience*, Dr. Tony Evans explains that all of life must be stewarded because all of life is under God.

After viewing Tony Evans' presentation "The Spheres," use the following questions to help you think through what you saw and heard.

1. How has the idea that stewardship pertains to all of life rather than just money challenged the understanding of stewardship you may have previously held?

2. Brainstorm a list of specific areas of life that should be stewarded under God's rule. Come up with as many areas as you can.

Dr. Evans taught that life can be separated into four spheres: individual, family, church, and community. On the following page, categorize each item from your list into its appropriate sphere. Let this exercise help you brainstorm additional areas of life that should be stewarded.

Individual   **Family**

Church   **Community**

3. Psalm 128 teaches the kingdom steward to fear God. To fear
    God is to take Him seriously. How does stewarding oneself
    demonstrate a fear of God?

How can you better steward yourself for God's glory?

4. What does Psalm 128:3-4 teach about stewarding one's family?

What are the results when a family is stewarded well?

5. In what ways do Satan's attacks on the family negatively impact society?

How does good stewardship counter Satan's attacks on the family?

6. How does understanding responsible stewardship of the home affect your view on family relationships?

7. Psalm 128:5 teaches the kingdom steward to manage his or her role in their place of worship. In today's world, this would apply to the local church. What is the purpose of the church?

For what purposes are we to be engaged in our local church?

8. What does the church do well? What does the church need to do better?

9. If Christians took seriously the job of stewarding their involvement in church, what would church look like?

What impact would this have on God's kingdom and on the world?

10. Many Christians have a tendency to pull away from society, but Jeremiah 29:6-7 reveals God's instructions to be productive stewards in the community. Read Jeremiah 29:6-7. How were the Israelites to be involved in the community?

What does God say will be the result of this involvement?

11. How could this spiritual principle apply to kingdom stewards who work in their communities today?

12. Share ideas of how kingdom stewards can practically invest in the local community today.

Transformation Moments

Read the following passages. Answer the questions that follow. If you run out of time, finish this section at home.

> How blessed is everyone who fears the LORD, who walks in His ways. When you shall eat of the fruit of your hands, you will be happy and it will be well with you.
>
> PSALM 128:1-2

Explain the happiness that comes when the kingdom steward fears the Lord.

Your wife shall be like a fruitful vine within your house, your children like olive plants around your table. Behold, for thus shall the man be blessed who fears the LORD.

PSALM 128:3-4

Whether you are married or single, what is one way you can better steward your household for God's glory?

The LORD bless you from Zion, and may you see the prosperity of Jerusalem all the days of your life. Indeed, may you see your children's children. Peace be upon Israel!

PSALM 128:5-6

How can you pray for the prosperity of your community, state, or country this week?

Final Challenge

A responsible kingdom steward rightfully aligns all of life under God's rule. This begins with the individual life, then expands to include the family, church, and community. In what ways can you broaden your personal prayer time to more fully cover all of these areas you are to steward?

4

✤

THE PERSPECTIVE

But godliness actually is a means of great gain when accompanied by contentment.

1 TIMOTHY 6:6

The Main Point

The perspective of the kingdom steward is to contentedly enjoy the abundance God gives while using it to benefit others and bring glory to God.

The Gathering

Begin your time together with prayer and praise. Seek to create a community of connection within your group by sharing prayer requests and experiences that provide members with an opportunity to engage with one another.

To find out more about how to cultivate a mindset of contentment, read the following excerpt from *Kingdom Stewardship*. Then discuss the question that appears at the end of the excerpt.

KINGDOM STEWARDS MIX GODLINESS
WITH CONTENTMENT

[First Timothy 6:6] serves as a great insight into the perspective we are to have as a kingdom steward. It says, "But godliness actually is a means of great gain when accompanied by contentment."

So much wisdom is packed in this one statement. Friend, if you want to truly live a rich life, you must learn how to mix godliness with contentment. Paul gives us a process for achieving great gains in our life, and that formula is: **godliness + contentment = great gain**. Combining these two things increases results—otherwise known as "great gain." Keep in mind, great gain here does not mean great material gain. It is referring to what I mentioned earlier as "true riches." Yes, that might include money but it also might not mean money.

Godliness is simply a lifestyle in which one seeks to please God. To live a godly life involves consistently reflecting the character of God in all that you do and say. It means remaining in the midst of God's presence. Now, a person can embody godliness but not achieve great gain when godliness is not coupled with contentment. When the motivation and parameters only focus on rules, rules, rules—all the while failing to include the essential element of contentment—a person can actually become paralyzed in their growth. This can quickly morph into pharisaical limitations constrained by pride, doubt, and endless effort. Godliness must be married to contentment if it is to produce great gain.

Knowing the opposite of something can often help us better understand what it is. The opposite of godliness is ungodliness. The opposite of contentment is discontentment. When we reverse the statement Paul made in this passage, we discover that ungodliness combined with discontentment results in great loss. This loss is the loss of "true riches" God supplies. True riches show up in a variety of ways, not just monetarily. These riches, however, always allow us to experience God's reality in our lives and circumstances.

Thus, the amount of true riches you gain or lose in life is largely up to you. Are you seeking to live a life that honors the presence and rule of the Lord Jesus Christ each day, or are you seeking to please yourself according to the world's system of values? How you answer that question will have a direct impact on both the quality and legacy of your life.[1]

Reflection and Discussion

Dr. Evans contrasts two perspectives on life:

godliness + contentment = great gain
ungodliness + discontentment = great loss

Describe the difference between living with each of these perspectives. How does the first perspective benefit the kingdom steward?

Show Time!

In session 4 of the *Kingdom Stewardship Group Video Experience,* Dr. Tony Evans speaks about contentment, loving God more than money, and the need to handle abundance properly.

After viewing Tony Evans' presentation "The Perspective," use the following questions to help you think through what you saw, read, and heard.

1. Dr. Evans taught that the first perspective that benefits a kingdom steward comes from 1 Timothy 6:6: **godliness + contentment = great gain.** Define godliness, contentment, and great gain.

Read Philippians 4:11. How does a person learn to be content?

What experiences in your life have taught you contentment?

2. For what purpose are we to be content?

What obstacles to contentment do people face today?

3. Read 1 Timothy 6:9-10. Dr. Evans said the second perspective
    is to not make money your highest goal, but rather to love
    God more than money. Why is this perspective important for
    kingdom stewards?

4. Dr. Evans contrasted several things in the video to illustrate the
    difference between material riches and spiritual riches. Describe
    the differences between the following examples he gave:

Material riches	Spiritual riches
A house	A home
Medicine	Healing

Friends   Authentic relationships

How can loving God more than money contribute to
acquiring spiritual riches rather than material riches?

5. Consider your view of money and your devotion to God.
    Do you need to rebalance your affections to put God above
    money? Explain.

6. The third perspective is to enjoy the abundance God has
    given you and to be generous with it. What does it mean to
    properly enjoy the abundance God gives?

7. Dr. Evans suggests that kingdom stewards be rich in good works and share with others. What does it mean to be rich in good works?

Why is it important to share with others?

What problems arise when people choose not to share out of their abundance?

8. Identify something of value that you own and make a decision to share it (by loaning it or giving it away) with someone else who may need it this week. If you can identify more than one item, all the better.

Why did you choose what you did?

In what way do you feel it will benefit someone else?

In what way will sharing this item benefit you and bring God glory?

Transformation Moments

Read the following passages. Answer the questions that follow. If you run out of time, finish this section at home.

> For we have brought nothing into the world, so we cannot take anything out of it either. If we have food and covering, with these we shall be content.
>
> I TIMOTHY 6:7-8

Focus on gratitude this week during your prayer time. Pay attention to how gratitude affects your level of contentment throughout the week.

> But those who want to get rich fall into temptation and a snare and many foolish and harmful desires which plunge men into ruin and destruction. For the love of money is a root of all sorts of evil, and some by longing for it have wandered away from the faith and pierced themselves with many griefs.
>
> I TIMOTHY 6:9-10

Make a list of different kinds of "evil" the love of money can lead to. Circle any that may already apply to you. Ask God to either keep you from falling into these areas or deliver you from them.

Instruct those who are rich in this present world not to be conceited or to fix their hope on the uncertainty of riches, but on God, who richly supplies us with all things to enjoy.

1 TIMOTHY 6:17

How can you more fully fix your hope on God this week?

Final Challenge

King Solomon, at one time the wealthiest man in the world, said, "He who loves money will not be satisfied with money, nor he who loves abundance with its income" (Ecclesiastes 5:10). One can be filled to overflowing with wealth and material possessions, but without an eternal perspective, this will result in craving for more and will likely end in many griefs. On the other hand, one can be the steward of God-given wealth and find peace, purpose, and contentment. Identify an area in your life in which it would be good for you to have greater contentment. Ask God to increase your contentment in this area this week.

5

THE MOTIVATION

*And God is able to make all grace abound to you, so that always having all
sufficiency in everything, you may have an abundance for every good deed.*

2 CORINTHIANS 9:8

The Main Point

God wants you to be a wise steward of all He has given to you
because of a heartfelt response to His grace and out of love for
Him.

The Gathering

Begin your time together with prayer and praise. Seek to create a
community of connection within your group by sharing prayer
requests and experiences that provide members with an opportunity to engage with one another.

To find out more about what should be a kingdom steward's
motivation for the wise management of resources, read the following excerpt from *Kingdom Stewardship*. Then discuss the question
that appears at the end of the excerpt.

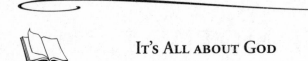

It's All about God

We're living in a day when people want God's blessings without God.

They want the benefits without the Being.

They want the rewards without the Relationship.

But that's all mixed up. That's backwards. That's similar to an extraordinary exchange in Scripture between God and Moses. Essentially, God told Moses that he was to take the Israelites into the Promised Land. He promised to send an angel before them in order to pave the way. He guaranteed the defeat of their enemies while simultaneously describing for Moses a land flowing with milk and honey. Bottom line: God told Moses that he and his people would receive guidance, protection, provision, and blessing.

But there is one thing God would not give them, due to their own obstinate ways: Himself. We read, "Go up to a land flowing with milk and honey; for I will not go up in your midst, because you are an obstinate people, and I might destroy you on the way" (Exodus 33:3).

The Israelites had been greenlit to go, with one caveat. They would go without God.

But Moses knew better than that.

Moses knew that the blessings of God were no match for the presence of God. He knew that milk and honey by the barrel meant nothing without the Source of that provision. Moses was wise enough to decline the offered blessings and push back with his own request,

> Now therefore, I pray You, if I have found favor in Your sight, let me know Your ways that I may know You, so that I may find favor in Your sight. Consider too, that this nation is Your people.
>
> EXODUS 33:13

God heard Moses' heart. He saw his motivation. Moses didn't strive for significance, success, or his own personal platform. If he did, this would have been his chance. Get God off to the sidelines, stick an angel in front, and push forward. Claim the land. Destroy the enemies. Drink the milk. Bathe in the honey. Go down in history as the greatest leader the Israelites—no, the world—had ever had.

But as I said earlier, Moses knew better than that. In fact, knowing better than that is why Moses was such a great leader after all. Moses had enough discernment to know that to go anywhere without God was foolishness. So, he didn't go on his own. More than that, he appealed to God's heart in his response, "Let me know Your ways that I may know You."

In other words, Moses made it clear that this wasn't just about knowing the strategies to build his nation's brand or establish his people as a dominant force. No, he let God know that the blessings without the

Blesser were no blessings at all. This was all about God: Loving Him. Knowing Him. Worshiping Him. Honoring Him. Experiencing Him. Journeying with Him. Understanding Him.[1]

Reflection and Discussion

What is the greatest insight you take away from the example of Moses refusing to go into the Promised Land without God?

Show Time!

In session 5 of the *Kingdom Stewardship Group Video Experience*, Dr. Tony Evans reminds us that grace is the greatest motivation for the wise stewardship of our resources.

After viewing Tony Evans' presentation "The Motivation," use the following questions to help you think through what you saw, read, and heard.

1. Dr. Evans said, "Grace is all that God is free to do for you which you could never do for yourself and that you could not earn, do not deserve, and could never repay." What are some examples of God's grace in your life?

   In what ways should God's grace motivate us to be kingdom stewards of our time, talents, and treasures?

2. Dr. Evans said that grace cannot be earned, but it can be accessed. What does he mean by this?

   How can a kingdom steward access God's grace?

3. Dr. Evans taught that just as the farmer sows seed (which comes from God), kingdom stewards are to sow grace (which comes from God). What does it mean to sow grace?

Where, how, and why are we to sow grace?

4. Recall a time when someone extended grace to you. Share that experience with the group. How did receiving grace from another affect you?

5. Describe what would happen if a farmer chose only to pray and did not plant any seeds. How does this apply to spiritual sowing and reaping as a kingdom steward?

6. In what ways does expecting a harvest motivate the farmer? In what ways does a kingdom steward sow grace with the motivation of reaping more grace?

7. Read Luke 6:38. What does Dr. Evans mean when he exhorts us to live as conduits of grace rather than as cul-de-sacs of grace?

8. Dr. Evans teaches that sowing and reaping happen in season and that there is a gap between seasons. How does this relate to spiritual stewardship?

    How can an awareness of a gap between sowing and reaping increase both your patience and diligence when it comes to extending grace to others?

9. How has God lavished grace on you? How can you extend that grace to others this week?

Transformation Moments

Read the following passages. Answer the questions that follow. If you run out of time, finish this section at home.

> Each one must do just as he has purposed in his heart, not grudgingly or under compulsion, for God loves a cheerful giver.
>
> 2 CORINTHIANS 9:7

This week, pick an amount to cheerfully give, however big or small. After you give, thank God for blessing you with abundance.

> Give, and it will be given to you. They will pour into your lap a good measure—pressed down, shaken together, and running over. For by your standard of measure it will be measured to you in return.
>
> LUKE 6:38

Choose to listen attentively to someone who needs a borrowed ear this week, and see how this is returned to you.

> But He gives a greater grace. Therefore it says, "God is opposed to the proud, but gives grace to the humble."
>
> JAMES 4:6

Is there an area of your life that causes you to be proud? In what ways have you experienced God "opposing" you in this area? Ask God to give you humility.

Final Challenge

> And God is able to make all grace abound to you, so that always having all sufficiency in everything, you may have an abundance for every good deed.
>
> 2 CORINTHIANS 9:8

The good that we do comes directly from God. He gives grace for us to have the sufficiency we need to do good works. Grace supplies the desire, motivation, power, insight, and skill for us to carry out His will. Think of something you want to do for God but that seems difficult. Pray 2 Corinthians 9:8 to God, thanking Him for the grace He's giving you to empower you to accomplish this good work. Ask God to use His grace to motivate you to do what He is asking you to do.

6

THE PRIORITY

But seek first His kingdom and His righteousness,
and all these things will be added to you.

MATTHEW 6:33

The Main Point

The priority of a kingdom steward must always be putting God first.

The Gathering

Begin your time together with prayer and praise. Seek to create a community of connection within your group by sharing prayer requests and experiences that provide members with an opportunity to engage with one another.

To find out more about the kingdom steward's priority, read the following excerpt from *Kingdom Stewardship*. Then discuss the question that appears at the end of the excerpt.

GOD CANNOT BE SECOND

Did you know there are certain things God cannot do? Now, before you close this book and start writing me an email with words like "heresy" in it, let me explain myself. I understand that the common thought is that God can do everything. But that's not entirely true. There exist some things God simply cannot do.

For example, God cannot lie. God exists as truth, embodies truth, and can speak only truth. Lying sits outside of His ability and nature (Hebrews 6:18). God cannot contradict His core character.

Another thing God cannot do is stop being God. He is the same in His essential Being and attributes yesterday, today, and forever (Hebrews 13:8). He also cannot sin or cause us to sin (James 1:13), due to the purity of His own makeup. Holiness and sinfulness cannot abide together, thus God cannot provoke sin in His own children within whom He resides.

See, there are a number of things God cannot do. One more thing He cannot do is He can't be second. God must be first. Always first. Never second, and certainly not less than that either. Yet unfortunately today we live in a world where most people, particularly in western culture, acknowledge God but do not give Him the position He deserves. They do not make Him first. First in their thoughts. First in their hearts. First in their priorities. First in their choices. First.

If you'll do a search of Scripture, it won't take you long to find places where God is demanding to be put first. In fact, the word "first" pops up a lot in the Bible—in relationship to God. For an example of this, see Matthew 6:33. God literally audits His position in people's lives. He won't take your word for it. Just because someone says God is first in his or her life doesn't mean God believes it. He audits each of us to see if He truly does hold the placement of first over all else.[1]

Reflection and Discussion

Why is it that God must be first and cannot be second?

Show Time!

In session 6 of the *Kingdom Stewardship Group Video Experience,* Dr. Tony Evans reminds us that God must be first in our finances and in our lives.

After viewing Tony Evans' presentation "The Priority," use the following questions to help you think through what you saw, read, and heard.

1. Dr. Evans said that God deserves and demands to be first in all things. Create a list of reasons God deserves to be first in the kingdom steward's life.

    Describe what it would look like for a kingdom steward to put God first in all areas of life.

2. In what ways do Christians fail to put God first?

    Why do Christians fail to put God first?

3. Dr. Evans taught that God developed the system of the tithe to reveal whether His people were putting Him first. Explain what Dr. Evans means by this.

4. The Bible talks about giving God "firstfruits" as a way of giving to Him financially. What does the Bible mean by firstfruits? What does giving firstfruits mean in today's culture?

5. Dr. Evans also mentioned the notion of giving God our leftovers. Do you give God firstfruits, leftovers, or a mixture of both? Explain.

6. Dr. Evans showed in Malachi 3 that God told the Israelites they were "robbing" Him. How were they robbing God?

In what ways might we be robbing God today?

7. In the video, Dr. Evans made the point that economic problems are sometimes tied to spiritual theft. Explain what this means.

What other kinds of problems might arise for the kingdom steward who fails to put God first in all things?

8. Dr. Evans said, "When you rob God, you rob yourself." What does this mean and how does it impact your view on honoring God first in all things?

9. Create a list of practical ways you can put God first in all things. Pray about this list. Share with the rest of the group the steps you will take to put God first in your life.

Transformation Moments

Read the following passages. Answer the questions that follow. If you run out of time, finish this section at home.

On the first day of every week each one of you is to put aside and save, as he may prosper, so that no collections be made when I come.

I CORINTHIANS 16:2

Set aside a place (jar, envelope, container) where you can place what you will be giving to God. Let this tangible and visual action encourage you and others to give to God regularly, generously, and cheerfully. Why is it important to encourage others to give through our example?

Honor the LORD from your wealth and from the first of all your produce; so your barns will be filled with plenty and your vats will overflow with new wine.

PROVERBS 3:9-10

What is the result of honoring God with the firstfruits of all you have?

You shall eat in the presence of the LORD your God, at the place where He chooses to establish His name, the tithe of your grain, your new wine, your oil, and the firstborn of

your herd and your flock, so that you may learn to fear the
LORD your God always.

DEUTERONOMY 14:23

How does the contemporary church use gifts given to God to
help others both locally and globally? What are some other ways
you'd like to see the church use its resources to invest in the well-
being of others?

Final Challenge

God deserves to be first in all areas of your life. Prayerfully consider
how you can make God first through the use of your time, through
the use of your talents, and through the use of your treasure. Take
steps to adjust your life to reflect this priority.

7

❧

THE REWARDS

Offer to God a sacrifice of thanksgiving and pay your vows to the Most High; call upon Me in the day of trouble; I shall rescue you, and you will honor Me.

PSALM 50:14-15

The Main Point

A kingdom steward can expect to receive a variety of rewards from God both in time and in eternity.

The Gathering

Begin your time together with prayer and praise. Seek to create a community of connection within your group by sharing prayer requests and experiences that provide members with an opportunity to engage with one another.

To find out more about the rewards of kingdom stewardship, read the following excerpt from *Kingdom Stewardship*. Then discuss the question that appears at the end of the excerpt.

GOD'S REWARDS PROGRAM

Airlines have rewards programs. These are programs designed to get you to fly more by giving you rewards for booking flights and purchasing items from their online shop. Usually you are awarded miles that allow you to fly virtually free due to your ongoing choice of them as your airline provider.

In the world of sports, athletes are offered what are known as incentive clauses. These are clauses designed to increase their productivity by motivating them to accomplish more. More yardage, catches, tackles, or any other detailed item in the incentive clause is rewarded with more money. This serves as motivation to keep the athletes playing at their highest potential throughout the course of a season.

Salvation is free. I don't want to skip over that. Salvation is by grace alone apart from works, through personal faith in the finished work of Jesus Christ and His promise to give eternal life to all who believe in Him for it (Romans 3:24; 4:4-5; Galatians 2:16, 21; Ephesians 2:8-9; Revelation 22:17). You can't buy it, earn it, or work for it because God will only give it away for free. As Titus 3:5 states, "He saved us, not on the basis of deeds which we have done in righteousness, but according to His mercy, by the washing of regeneration and renewing by the Holy Spirit."

But once a person is born again, God has an incentive clause. He has a rewards program. Keep in mind, the rewards program has nothing to do with the security of your eternal destiny because that's a free gift from God.

But the rewards program has everything to do with how much of heaven you get to experience on earth as well as your kingdom inheritance when you get to glory. God's rewards program, unlike eternal salvation, is based on a faith that works—not faith apart from works (James 2:14-21).

God wants you to maximize your potential on earth and to increase His engagement with your life. He seeks to do this by incentivizing what you do. In fact, God has laid out seven* specific incentives for you to aim for as you manage the time, talents, and treasures He has placed within your realm of kingdom stewardship. These seven potential rewards do not come to believers simply because they are Christians. It's only when you, as a kingdom steward, rightly position yourself in God's kingdom program through the choices you make that they will be made available to you.[1]

---

* While Dr. Evans discusses seven incentives or rewards in the *Kingdom Stewardship* book, he focuses on four of these rewards in the video segment. The discussion in this session will focus on the four rewards mentioned in the video.

Reflection and Discussion

Why does God reward those who are wise stewards of their time, talents, and treasures?

Show Time!

In session 7 of the *Kingdom Stewardship Group Video Experience*, Dr. Tony Evans reminds us that God rewards those who rightly align their thoughts, words, and actions under His rule.

After viewing Tony Evans' presentation "The Rewards," use the following questions to help you think through what you saw, read, and heard.

1. Dr. Evans makes it clear that the rewards he teaches about in this session are separate from the salvation we receive in Christ. Read Titus 3:5. Briefly explain the process of salvation.

2. In what ways are the rewards that kingdom stewards receive different from salvation?

3. Why is it important to know that God rewards faithful stewardship both in this lifetime and in eternity?

4. In your own words, define the four rewards for living faithfully as a kingdom steward and review what Dr. Evans taught about them.

Answered Prayer:

Met Needs:

Emotional Stability:

Divine Guidance:

5. Which of these four rewards means the most to you? Why?

6. Have you personally experienced any of these benefits? Share your experience with the rest of the group.

7. How do the four listed rewards contribute to the fulfillment of each other?

8. What are some additional benefits for living as a kingdom steward that weren't mentioned in this week's video lesson?

9. What can you discern about the nature and character of God
    from His practice of rewarding faithful stewardship?

Transformation Moments

Read the following passages. Answer the questions that follow. If
you run out of time, finish this section at home.

> But I have received everything in full and have an
> abundance; I am amply supplied, having received from
> Epaphroditus what you have sent, a fragrant aroma, an
> acceptable sacrifice, well-pleasing to God. And my God
> will supply all your needs according to His riches in glory
> in Christ Jesus.
>
> PHILIPPIANS 4:18-19

How are giving to others and God meeting your own needs con-
nected? What spiritual benefits can you gain by giving to others?

I have been young and now I am old, yet I have not seen
the righteous forsaken or his descendants begging bread.

PSALM 37:25

Describe how it makes you feel to know that God will never for-
sake or abandon His people.

It is the blessing of the LORD that makes rich, and He adds
no sorrow to it.

PROVERBS 10:22

Identify any areas of provision in your life that do not seem
accompanied with peace or joy. Ask God for wisdom on how to
adjust your thinking or actions in order to get in alignment under
Him in those areas.

Final Challenge

Isaiah 48:17-18 tells us that God teaches us which way we are to go. His guidance brings about profit and productivity. This reward of divine guidance can set you on the path toward personal growth and development. This week, ask God not only for His guidance but also for Him to show you how better to align yourself under Him so that you can access this reward more fully.

8

🌿

THE STRATEGY

*And his master praised the unrighteous manager because he had
acted shrewdly; for the sons of this age are more shrewd in relation
to their own kind than the sons of light.*

LUKE 16:8

The Main Point
A kingdom steward strategically uses all of his or her resources
(time, talents, and treasures) to actively advance God's kingdom
on earth.

The Gathering
Begin your time together with prayer and praise. Seek to create a
community of connection within your group by sharing prayer
requests and experiences that provide members with an opportunity to engage with one another.

To find out more about a kingdom steward's strategy, read the
following excerpt from *Kingdom Stewardship*. Then discuss the
question that appears at the end of the excerpt.

  ## Your Strategy for Abundant Life

Jesus is telling you and me to cover our future (both earthly and eternal) through our strategic decisions in our present. We are to invest in our future by strategically operating in our present environment. One day money is going to fail you. For example, if the doctor says a person has a terminal illness, money cannot change that. Money can't bail a person out of everything. There will always be situations in your life that money can't buy a person out of. Eventually, it loses its power. It loses its potency. It loses its ability to resolve the problems. Or it simply runs out or is destroyed (2 Peter 3:10). If you put all of your eggs in the money basket, you will eventually find yourself in a lot of trouble and without any resources when money fails. . . .

Jesus didn't share [the story of the shrewd manager] to tell you how to get rich on earth, though. He shared this parable to illustrate how to think strategically for your eternal future. When you leave this life and head into eternity, there will be an opportunity for a Welcoming Committee. The question is how many people are going to be at the pearly gate to welcome you because of the impact you made on their lives spiritually.

Did you disciple, mentor, and guide others on how to have their sin debt paid in full through the death, burial, and resurrection of Jesus Christ? Did you show others how to profit spiritually on earth by overcoming Satan's schemes? Did you use your time, talents, and treasures shrewdly in order to help others experience a greater level of spiritual productivity themselves?

Jesus is calling you to strategically prioritize the spiritual over the material. He uses the material (money) to teach a point about the spiritual. As we read further in Luke 16, this distinction is clearly made. "No servant can serve two masters; for either he will hate the one and love the other, or else he will be devoted to one and despise the other. You cannot serve God and wealth" (verse 13).

By showing the tangible connection between the unrighteous steward's present with his future, Jesus is trying to help us make a mental connection between our present and our future as well. When a person fails to be strategic with their time, talents, and treasures on earth as a steward for God's kingdom purposes, that person will reach the time of accounting on Judgment Day and have nothing to show for it. Yes, salvation is free, based on faith alone in Christ alone. But rewards come tied to what you do on earth.[1]

Reflection and Discussion

Why is it important to be strategic in how we live as kingdom stewards?

Show Time!

In this last session of the *Kingdom Stewardship Group Video Experience*, Dr. Tony Evans teaches that God instructs us to use the resources He's given strategically for the advancement of His kingdom.

After viewing Tony Evans' presentation "The Strategy," use the following questions to help you think through what you saw, read, and heard.

1. What is the definition of kingdom stewardship? Refer back to session 1 if you need to.

Rewrite this definition in your own words and share it with the group. Explain your reasons for wording the definition as you did.

2. Consider what you've learned about kingdom stewardship during this course. Tell the group how your thinking has changed during these sessions.

3. Dr. Evans taught about the parable of the shrewd manager from Luke 16:1-13. Review the parable and summarize how the manager strategically built relationships to change his future prospects.

Are you surprised that Jesus used an unrighteous steward as an example for how we are to strategically manage resources in His kingdom? Why or why not?

4. Dr. Evans said, "Unbelievers seize opportunities to progress in their lives through the relationships that they build. You cut deals on golf courses—big deals. The purpose of the golf course is to establish the relationship. Jesus says that unrighteous people know how to do that when righteous people don't." What lessons can be learned about using strategy for kingdom purposes?

5. The shrewd manager made mistakes. What boundaries must the kingdom steward consider in developing strategies for kingdom work?

6. In what way can acts of service and relationship-building be done strategically for kingdom purposes?

7. Describe other ways kingdom stewards can live shrewdly with regard to good works.

8. How does Satan use oppositional thoughts and wrong perspectives to keep Christians from living strategically?

9. Dr. Evans ends this video session by saying that one day this life will end. He teaches that it's not what we leave behind that will matter. Rather, it's what we've "forwarded ahead" to eternity that will matter. Dr. Evans challenges us to strategically use what God has entrusted to us to make a difference for eternity. What will you do to develop an eternal kingdom perspective and live strategically as a kingdom steward?

Transformation Moments

Read the following passages. Answer the questions that follow. If you run out of time, finish this section at home.

> If any of you lacks wisdom, let him ask of God, who gives to all generously without reproach, and it will be given to him.
>
> JAMES 1:5

In what way can you gain greater insight into living strategically through the practice of prayer?

> But sanctify Christ as Lord in your hearts, always being ready to make a defense to everyone who asks you to give an account for the hope that is in you, yet with gentleness and reverence.
>
> 1 PETER 3:15

How can you strategically plan to make a difference for eternity with the words you speak to others?

As each one has received a special gift, employ it in serving one another as good stewards of the manifold grace of God. Whoever speaks, is to do so as one who is speaking the utterances of God; whoever serves is to do so as one who is serving by the strength which God supplies; so that in all things God may be glorified through Jesus Christ, to whom belongs the glory and dominion forever and ever. Amen.

I PETER 4:10-11

How can you make the best use of all the resources God has given you in order to protect and expand God's assets and bring Him glory?

Final Challenge

Ask God to open your eyes and heart to opportunities to serve others and develop relationships through your normal routines of life, so that you might impact them for the kingdom. Keep a journal of these experiences and reflect on how God is growing and developing you in the strategic use of your life, for His glory and the advancement of His kingdom.

Acknowledgments

I want to thank my friends at Focus on the Family and Tyndale House Publishers for their long-standing partnership in bringing my thoughts, study, and words to print. I particularly want to thank Larry Weeden for his friendship over the years, as well as his pursuit of excellence in the Kingdom line of books and materials. I also want to publicly thank Steve Johnson, Allison Montjoy, Beth Robinson, and Whitney Harrison for their work in getting this book into the marketplace. In addition, my appreciation goes out to Heather Hair for her skills and insights in collaboration on this manuscript.

Notes

SESSION 1: THE RESPONSIBILITY
1. Tony Evans, *Kingdom Stewardship* (Carol Stream, IL: Focus on the Family/Tyndale House Publishers, 2020), 7–9.

SESSION 2: THE COVENANT
1. Tony Evans, *Kingdom Stewardship* (Carol Stream, IL: Focus on the Family/Tyndale House Publishers, 2020), 76–77.

SESSION 3: THE SPHERES
1. Tony Evans, *Kingdom Stewardship* (Carol Stream, IL: Focus on the Family/Tyndale House Publishers, 2020), 90–92.

SESSION 4: THE PERSPECTIVE
1. Tony Evans, *Kingdom Stewardship* (Carol Stream, IL: Focus on the Family/Tyndale House Publishers, 2020), 150–152.

SESSION 5: THE MOTIVATION
1. Tony Evans, *Kingdom Stewardship* (Carol Stream, IL: Focus on the Family/Tyndale House Publishers, 2020), 46–47.

SESSION 6: THE PRIORITY
1. Tony Evans, *Kingdom Stewardship* (Carol Stream, IL: Focus on the Family/Tyndale House Publishers, 2020), 129–130.

SESSION 7: THE REWARDS
1. Tony Evans, *Kingdom Stewardship* (Carol Stream, IL: Focus on the Family/Tyndale House Publishers, 2020), 189–190.

SESSION 8: THE STRATEGY
1. Tony Evans, *Kingdom Stewardship* (Carol Stream, IL: Focus on the Family/Tyndale House Publishers, 2020), 114–117.

About Dr. Tony Evans

Dr. Tony Evans is the founder and senior pastor of Oak Cliff Bible Fellowship in Dallas, founder and president of The Urban Alternative, chaplain of the NBA's Dallas Mavericks, and author of over 100 books, booklets, and Bible studies. The first African American to earn a doctorate of theology from Dallas Theological Seminary, he has been named one of the 12 Most Effective Preachers in the English-Speaking World by Baylor University.

Dr. Evans holds the honor of writing and publishing the first full-Bible commentary and study Bible by an African American.

His radio broadcast, *The Alternative with Dr. Tony Evans*, can be heard on more than 1,400 US outlets daily and in more than 130 countries.